FISHING

BEARS

by Ruth Berman
photographs by Lynn M. Stone

 HOUGHTON MIFFLIN BOSTON • MORRIS PLAINS, NJ

California • Colorado • Georgia • Illinois • New Jersey • Texas

Additional photographs reproduced with permission:
© Glenn M. Oliver, Visuals Unlimited, p. 20 (inset);
© Rick McIntyre, p. 24.

Fishing Bears, by Ruth Berman, photographs by Lynn
M. Stone. Text copyright © 1998 by Ruth Berman.
Photographs copyright © 1998 by Lynn M. Stone
except as noted. Reprinted by arrangement with the
publisher, Lerner Publications, Minneapolis,
Minnesota. All rights reserved.

Houghton Mifflin Edition, 2005

Printed in the U.S.A.

ISBN: 0-618-06194-0

789-B-06 05 04 03

These are brown bear tracks. How many toe marks can you count?

This is an Alaskan brown bear.

Alaskan brown bears live near water.

They have small ears, small eyes,
and a big long nose.

Bears can stand up on their hind legs.

This mother bear stands to smell
the air for food and for enemies.

Mother bears usually have *twins* or *triplets*.

Baby bears are called *cubs*.

Cubs stay with their mothers
for one to three years.

This cub is napping on Mom!

These cubs are playing.

Brown bears are *omnivores*.

Omnivores are animals that eat both plants and animals.

Are you an omnivore?

Most furry animals walk on their toes.

Bears walk with their feet
flat on the ground.

These bears are walking on a trail.

The trail ends at a river. Brown
bears look for fish in rivers.

Look! These bears are fighting
over a good fishing spot.

The bigger bear wins. It is
about to catch a *salmon!*

What do you think this bear is doing?

It is fishing for salmon
under the water.

These bears are *pouncing* on salmon.

Can you find a mother and
her cubs in this picture?

The mother is keeping her cubs
safe from a male bear.

This small bear is trying to sneak
some food!

Alaskan brown bears also eat *clams*.

Bears have to dig for clams.

Alaskan brown bears get ready
for winter by eating a lot.

Eating a lot makes them fat.

Why do bears need to get fat?

Fat keeps them warm and healthy during the winter.

Brown bears stay in *dens* for most of the winter. A brown bear is *hibernating* in this cozy den.

When bears hibernate, they are in a deep sleep.

In the spring, bears leave their dens
to look for food.

Then bears eat and eat.

They will be fat again
by next winter.

Fishing is hard work!
It is time to rest.

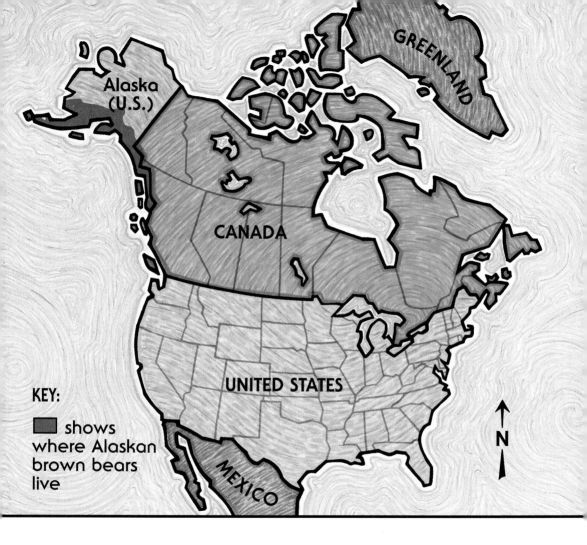

KEY:

■ shows where Alaskan brown bears live

Alaska (U.S.)

GREENLAND

CANADA

UNITED STATES

MEXICO

N

Find your state or province on this map.
Do Alaskan brown bears live near you?

Parts of a Brown Bear's Body

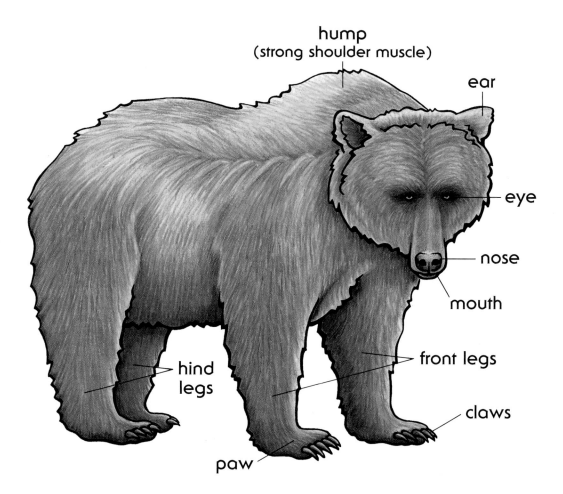

hump
(strong shoulder muscle)

ear

eye

nose

mouth

front legs

claws

hind
legs

paw

Glossary

clams: boneless animals that live inside a shell. (Clams are found under wet sand or mud. The soft meat of a clam can be eaten.)

cubs: baby bears

dens: cozy, safe places to live

hibernating: spending most of the winter in a deep sleep

omnivores: animals that eat both plants and animals

pouncing: jumping onto something suddenly

salmon: a kind of large fish

triplets: three babies born at one time to the same mother

twins: two babies born at one time to the same mother

Hunt and Find

The publisher wishes to extend special thanks to our **series consultant,** Sharyn Fenwick. An elementary science-math specialist, Mrs. Fenwick was the recipient of the National Science Teachers Association 1991 Distinguished Teaching Award. In 1992, representing the state of Minnesota at the elementary level, she received the Presidential Award for Excellence in Math and Science Teaching.

Robin Buckley

About the Author

Ruth Berman was born in New York and grew up in Minnesota. As a child, she spent her time going to school and saving lost and hurt animals. Later, Ruth volunteered at three zoos and got her degree in English. She enjoys writing science books for children. She has written six books in Lerner's Pull Ahead series. Her other books include *Ants, Peacocks,* and *My Pet Dog* (Lerner Publications) and *Sharks* and *American Bison* (Carolrhoda Books). Ruth lives in California with her husband Andy, dog Hannah, and her two cats Nikki and Toby.

About the Photographer

Lynn M. Stone is the author and photographer of many nature books for young readers, including *Cougars, Penguins, Sandhill Cranes,* and *Swans* (Lerner Publications). He is also the photographer of *Tigers* and *Vultures* (Lerner Publications). In addition to photographing wildlife, Mr. Stone enjoys fishing and traveling. A former teacher, he lives with his wife and daughter in Batavia, Illinois.